Lancasters Lake

The swamp that grew into one of Sunland's treasured landmarks.

**The Early History of Sunland, California
Volume 6**

ML Tiernan

Lancasters Lake

www.maryleetiernan.com
Second printing April 1, 2015
10 9 8 7 6 5 4 3 2

ISBN 978-0983067252 (Paperback)

©1999 ©2010 MaryLee Tiernan. All rights reserved. No portion of this product may be photographed, scanned, translated, reproduced, copied, or reduced to any tangible or electronic medium or machine-readable form, without the prior written consent of Mary Lee Tiernan.

Photograph on cover courtesy of Bolton Hall Museum, Tujunga, California.

Contents

The Family 5

The Lake 15

Map of Lancasters Lake 31

Footnotes 32

Bibliography 33

The Early History of Sunland, California series 36

Author's Notes

The researcher, like a detective, examines the evidence to try to determine the real story. Unfortunately for researchers, we cannot re-examine witnesses or revisit scenes because in most cases, they have long since disappeared. So we sort through the conflicting data to find the most reliable and logical explanations. I have done my best to follow the clues and weave as authentic a story as possible.

My thanks to the staff at Bolton Hall Museum, Tujunga, California, for their assistance with this project.

The Family

With only a dozen or so families living in Sunland, the addition of six more people named Lancaster shouldn't have posed a problem. So when Margaret sent her youngsters off to school, she probably looked forward to a day of unpacking without her four children underfoot. How much easier that would be! Imagine her astonishment

The Lancasters' first home on Sherman Grove Avenue circa 1922.
Photo courtesy of Marshall Murray.

when William, Paul, Marie, and Irene appeared back home only minutes later. The tiny, one-room schoolhouse had no room for them.

The arrival of the Lancaster family foreshadowed many changes for Sunland. The first, obviously, was to enlarge the schoolhouse an additional six feet to accommodate the new attendees. But what if other new students needed to be squeezed in? An extension only offered a temporary solution.

The need for a newer and larger school spawned Edgar Lancaster's leadership. He headed a movement to build one, and despite the opposition, he won. The next year, the new school, located on the northeast corner of Sunland Park, easily accommodated all the children in its one large room.

Edgar Lancaster had operated a grocery store in Pasadena for many years. Customers normally paid for groceries by credit, not cash, by entering their names in a book on the counter. Fed up with trying to collect over-due bills, Edgar sold the store and initially bought five acres of land in Sunland just north of the park, on the west side of Sherman Grove Avenue. The purchase included a house, an orchard, a swamp, and enough pasture for a cow, horses, chickens, ducks, and a couple of hogs.

Edgar continued in the grocery business, but now as a

farmer, growing and selling the fruit from his orchard. Each day he drove fourteen miles to Pasadena to take his peaches to market, a trip that took three hours each way along a one-lane dirt road. Later the family bought an additional 20 acres, full of weeds and dead grapevines, east of Oro Vista and south of Foothill. After reviving the vineyard, Edgar or his son Paul delivered both grapes and peaches to the Pasadena markets. The trip improved after 1910, when the county paved the dirt road—then called Michigan Avenue, later renamed Foothill Boulevard—and widened it to 15 feet.

Edgar began digging out a swampy portion of his land.
Photo courtesy of Bolton Hall Museum.

Few businesses existed in Sunland when the Lancasters moved there, simply because not enough people lived in the valley to support many stores. And everyone attended the Free Methodist Church, the only church in town—until the arrival of the Lancasters, that is. When it came to attending Sunday school, Bill Lancaster protested. Attending a Methodist Sunday school didn't bother his Baptist upbringing; no, he refused on the basis that "only girls went there,"[1] and he wasn't going to get caught with just a bunch of girls.

Instead of arguing with him, Margaret and Edgar sent him out to round up his friends. That afternoon, the Lancasters held their own Sunday school with 11 boys in the front room of their home. The next Sunday, 29 people attended. Thus the Lancasters brought the Baptist Church to Sunland.

By the next year, the Sunday school outgrew the Lancaster living room and moved into the new schoolhouse for meetings. As the congregation expanded over the next ten years, the need for a church of their own became evident. Edgar and Dr. G.M. Hammond donated land on Eldora for the building of the Sunland Baptist Church, erected in 1925. But as pleased as the members were about their new church, they thought longingly of the one thing it lacked because the cost of building the church had depleted their fund. They wanted a bell.

Many of the movie studios filmed in and around Sunland in those early days. Abe Lincoln strode through Sunland Park[2], Zorro raced down Roscoe Boulevard[3], and

Claudette Colbert raised her skirt a few inches to hitch a ride[4], a provocative action at the time. The Lancasters became acquainted with yet another star, Mary Pickford, as several of her films were shot on their land. Grateful to the Lancasters for their hospitality, she graciously donated the bell for the new church. When the congregation moved to another location on Oro Vista in 1951, they brought the bell with them. It rang on Sunday mornings—once to signal the beginning of worship, and once more to signal the end.

**Fishing on the lake - probably in the late 1920s.
Photo courtesy of Bolton Hall Museum.**

The Lancaster home was typical of early Sunland: a fireplace for heat, kerosene lamps for light, a well for running water. Fruit from the orchard was eaten fresh, in season, or canned; family gardens provided vegetables. For meat, the menfolk might venture into the nearby hills and hunt, and mom usually raised poultry in the backyard. In a pinch, one could buy meat from the butcher who came to town once a week.

Although one could go to Los Angeles for needed supplies, the long trip precluded their going very often. For the most part, these self-reliant pioneers produced what they needed themselves, whether in terms of goods or know-how. For example, when electricity arrived in 1914, no utility truck pulled up in front to hookup the house to the lines. Residents installed their own wiring, which usually ran helter-skelter across the land. During inclement weather, the wiring often broke and residents followed the lines to locate the problems and make their own repairs.

1927 - early days at the lake. Photo courtesy of Marshall Murray.

Neighbors and family just naturally helped each other. It's hard to imagine that a half-hour car trip (traffic permitting) to Los Angeles in modern times took two days by horse in the early 1900s. When Clara and Alfred Blumfield, who lived across the street from the Lancasters, needed to go "to town," Margaret automatically invited their children into her home. She would later have to do the same for her own grandchildren.

During the devastating flu pandemic of 1918-1919, which affected 25 percent of the U.S. population and killed 20 million people world-wide, Margaret's daughter Irene and her husband Ivan both caught the flu. Irene and Ivan lived near Irene's sister Marie in Jerome, Arizona. When their baby, also named Irene, was only six weeks old, her

The northern end of the lake when one could drive up to the picnic area.

Aunt Marie brought her to California so her grandparents could care for her. To keep the baby safe during the train trip, Marie kept the baby in a picnic basket. That almost had the opposite effect, however, when a well-intentioned man tried to grab the basket as Marie struggled to board the train. "Be careful," she yelled, "there's a baby in there."[5] Mother Irene "went to meet the Lord," as brother Paul expressed it, but Ivan eventually recovered and later remarried.

All the children helped out with typical chores like milking the cows or feeding the chickens. Marie's contribution may have been the most unique. She gave English lessons two nights a week to five or six Japanese workers who picked olives in the Wright groves.

After her divorce in 1934, daughter Marie returned to Sunland with her children to live with Granpa[6] Lancaster. And the chores were still there—this time for the grandchildren—and this time at the lake.

"I was put in charge of the boats," said Marshall Murray. "I had to collect 35 cents for 30 minutes of rental time, call the boats in if they failed to come in on time, breakup water fights, and keep general law and order."[7] The hardest part, he admitted, was having to work when his friends came to the lake to play.

After eighth grade, the Lancaster children attended

Glendale High School. By 1913, an electric car ran between Glendale and Montrose. The kids caught a bus from Sunland to the end of the line in Montrose, took the electric car to Glendale, and caught another bus to the high school, usually getting there on time. When Paul graduated in 1917, eight Sunland students made this daily trip.

The long hours traveling back and forth to school and the chores at home didn't prevent the youngsters from enjoying themselves. Paul Lancaster and Elmer Adams liked to pile loose hay high on a big flat-top truck drawn by horses. They packed some picnic baskets, picked up friends and neighbors, and headed out for a day of fun. Inventive as their parents, someone usually brought along a homemade ukulele crafted from a wooden cigar box to accompany the singing. Four rubber bands, fastened with tacks, stretched across the length of the box for strings; a piece of straight wood formed the neck. And it did the job quite well.

At other times, the kids amused themselves with ice cream socials, rabbit hunting, Sunday school parties, corn roasts, taffy pulls, potato bakes, or plays in the park. And they didn't spend much time on the phone, especially since one line served the entire town and anyone could pick up the phone and listen in on their conversations.

The entrance to Lancasters Lake on Sherman Grove Avenue circa 1937 driving north from Sunland Park toward Wentworth Avenue.

Photo courtesy of Marshall Murray.

The Lake

The 1920s brought bobbed hair, the Charleston, and fringed flapper dresses to the rest of the world; to Sunland they brought Lancasters Lake.[8] After the death of his wife Margaret, or Maggie, in October 1922, Edgar was so depressed that he wanted to leave the ranch and never return. He traveled north to visit some of the wonders of the West, including Crater Lake. He did return to Sunland,

The lake circa 1931. Photo courtesy of Bolton Hall Museum.

but he was lonely and restless. His grandson Marshall Murray recalls, "He wanted something—something big and important. Crater Lake gave him the inspiration to make a lake from the wet area on the ranch. He thought that if he could scoop the mud out of the wet hollow, he might pump in enough water to fill up the hole and make a lake."[9]

Without the benefit of bulldozers or other mechanical diggers, early settlers scooped out the earth the hard way while clearing building sites. Along with the earth came the never-ending supply of rocks. These thrifty founders piled the rocks as berms for strong foundations or retaining walls, or constructed homes. Many of these original buildings and berms are still standing.

The museum housed an assortment of relics from pioneer days.
Photo courtesy of Marshall Murray.

On hot summer days, the children in town begged to go swimming in the new lake and the accommodating Lancasters consented. Girls could swim two days a week, boys the rest of the time, with a family member acting as lifeguard.

A solid rock hill north of Sunland Park, which prevented water run-off from draining into the ground, had originally created the wet hollow or swamp on the back of the Lancaster property. After Edgar's excavation, in addition to the water he pumped into the lake, water continued to seep naturally into the basin, filling it up, and

One of the cabins at the lake available for rent.
Photo courtesy of Marshall Murray.

Edgar kept digging it out. By 1924, the rustic lake covered two acres with a depth of about four feet.

Because of the muddy bottom, the lake was no longer suitable for swimming, although the kids "just sort of fell in"[10] when the hot sun blazed. Sunland Park remained the more popular spot for family picnics and outings, but the lake definitely attracted the kids who "went and hoped

The "snack shack" sold treats such as soda or ice cream but was also the place to rent a boat or a fishing pole.
Photo courtesy of Marshall Murray.

something fun happened."[11] For 25 years, locals and visitors flocked to it cool shores for a day of relaxation or adventure.

Edgar "Granpa" Lancaster
Photos courtesy of Marshall Murray.

The children's special playground with Edgar's handcarved animals to ride and miniature merry-go-rounds made from wagon wheels.

Most of the animals had leather ears and saddle,
a rope tail, a moveable head, and pop-bottle eyes.

Just opposite where Hillrose Street once dead-ended into 10711 Sherman Grove Avenue, two tall poles, standing at an angle from the road, marked the entrance to Lancasters Lake. Up the short, curved path on the left stood a small museum, constructed from rock. It housed discarded implements used by Sunland's earliest founders, wooden Indians carved by Edgar, an old pump organ, pachinko games, horse livery, old clothes, and movie memorabilia including an old-time moving-picture machine where one flipped individual pictures to make them 'move.' The windows, made from wagon wheels with colored glass inserted between the spokes, showered the inside of the museum with magical color. The contents of the museum 'disappeared' during the 1950s when the land was leased. Beyond the museum stood two or three small, picturesque cabins.

Young children dashed toward their own special play area on the right, with swings and miniature merry-go-rounds made from wagon wheels. The wheels were mounted on posts firmly planted in the ground. The kids sat on the wheels, held on to the spokes, and used their feet to spin the wheel round and round till they grew dizzy. For their pleasure, Edgar also carved animals from logs, the wood soon worn smooth from the loving touch of many small hands. Whether a rocking horse, buffalo, pig, elephant, or camel, each had leather ears and saddle, a rope tail, a moveable head, and pop-bottle eyes.

"Granpa Lancaster," as the children called him, may have been physically small in stature, but not in his love for children. Summer crowds at the lake thinned during the winter, so it was not too unusual to have the lake to oneself, especially on an overcast day. One of the children, who lived close by, decided to take her new puppy down to the lake to treat him to a ride in a rowboat. Only the puppy saw a squirrel and got so excited that he jumped up and down, tipping over the boat. When Granpa Lancaster came to the rescue, the child tearfully pleaded, "Please, don't tell my mother."[12] Edgar took the child into the snack shack, warmed up the old wood stove, and let child and puppy dry out before he sent them on their way. And he never did tell.

One reached the longer section of the lake first. At the very end, the picnic area included a pavilion, reminiscent of a little stage, used by one of the movie studios as a set for a fight scene in a Joe Lewis movie. Those interested in rowing or fishing walked north on the right side of the lake to rent a boat or a fishing pole at the snack shack, or treated themselves to soda-pop or ice cream. Edgar added rowboats to the lake in 1926; he named the original six after his grandchildren. Rowers guided the blue and green boats around the lake and under the arched stone bridge on the north end into a lagoon. The less ambitious just rowed out to the middle of the lake and drifted lazily, or settled back and cast their fishing lines.

The boats also tempted local boys who liked to play a harmless prank. Before the lake would open for the day, they would row the boats out to the tiny island on the south end of the lake and beach them, knowing full well that Paul Lancaster, pretending to be irate, would then come chasing after them with his shotgun.

The pavilion on the south end of the lake was used as a movie set.

The cattails growing around the lake prompted another prank when movie director D.W. Griffith was filming in

Sunland Park. Some of the boys gathered the cattails and brought them to the park where they pulled them, filling the air with slow-floating fluff. A furious Griffith had to "cut" and wait for the air to clear before he could resume filming.

In 1927, the Lancasters seeded the lake with 500 catfish. Visitors could rent a simple fishing pole: a long pole, sans reel, with bait attached on the end of the line. Tom Sawyer would have felt right at home. Catfish cost 25¢ for each one caught.

Lush weeping willows and lilies surrounded the shorter section of the lake, creating a lagoon. The setting also attracted movie studios that filmed at this cherished community spot, which is how the Lancasters came to know Mary Pickford. While filming at the lake, studios usually setup tents for the stars who welcomed visits from the local kids. A friendly Alan Ladd invited the kids into his tent for a chat, and Forest Tucker let the kids try on his diving helmet, a prop for a "deep-sea" movie. They couldn't move under the weight of the old-fashioned helmet.

Visitors relaxed at the picnic tables carved from tree trunks. They could simply sit back and watch swans glide gracefully across the water, or wave to friends out rowing, or wander down to the water's edge to feed the ducks. To the delight of birdwatchers, the luxurious greenery attracted 51 different species of birds. Those looking for some exercise walked around the lake on a dirt path—well, almost around the lake. The many trees and plants bordering the lagoon hindered clear passage, so walkers usually by-passed the lagoon by crossing over the bridge. Eucalyptus trees shaded the north portion of the lake. Hidden among the trees on the west side, a creek ran through a ravine, a spot that local children found especially enticing.

An unusual storm covered Sunland in snow and froze the lake
in January 1949.
Photo courtesy of Marshall Murray.

Perhaps the greatest attraction to local children was simply that the lake was there. It was their playground. If they didn't go the lake with friends, they went alone—someone they knew was sure to show up. If they didn't have the price of a rowboat or fishing pole, catching a polliwog was just as much fun. The ravine in back provided endless hours of exploring; the tiny island a perfect setting for playing marooned or Treasure Island. What their imaginations didn't supply, sometimes the movie studios did with their sets and stars—like Johnny Weissmuller fighting alligators by the bridge in one of his Tarzan movies.

Hollywood stars, however, can also deliver a harsh dose of reality. Marshall Murray recalls watching the filming of Tarzan. "I remember standing on the bridge that separated the two parts of the lake watching Tarzan stab an alligator with a rubber knife. A movie man saw me and said, 'Beat it, kid, you don't belong here.' I shouted back, 'I live here.' Johnny came out of the water wet and cold, and someone handed him a bottle of brandy. He took a couple of long drinks—there went my image of Tarzan!"[13]

The 25-year history of Lancasters Lake records only one disaster. Six-year-old Robert Lee Glover of Russett Avenue, Sunland, drowned in the lake in 1944, just a few years before the demise of the lake itself.

The construction of concrete drainage ditches from

Haines Canyon to the wash prevented water from seeping into the soil—water which had fed the lake. For a while, the family continued to pump water into the lake, but this, too, became a problem because the Adams Olive Cannery used water from the same pump, and there just wasn't enough water for both of them.

The bridge separated the two sections of the lake.
Photo courtesy of Bolton Hall Museum.

When Edgar had a stroke in 1949 and his grandson Marshall left for college, there was no one to care for the property. The water receded in the lake until it finally dried up around 1950. Health officials condemned the site as a breeding ground for mosquitoes and required the bed of the lake to be filled in. The demise of the lake foreshadowed that of its creator, Edgar Lancaster, who died in 1951 at the age of 93.

The Lancaster land was leased for a few years in the early 1950s. In 1954, John and Florence Plemmons bought it and renamed the site the Sherman Grove Park. Picnic grounds covered the old bed of the lake. Later the property was converted to the Sherman Grove Mobile Home Park, and the picnic tables became rows of house trailers.

#####

Map of Lancasters Lake

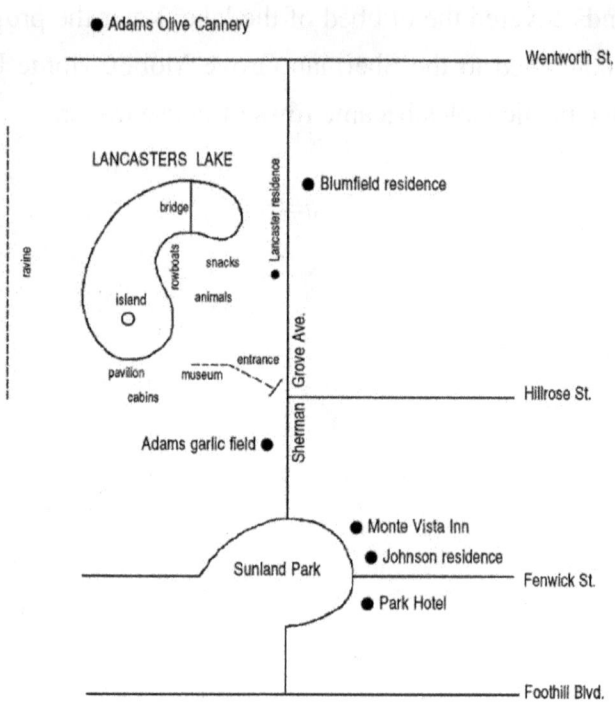

Footnotes

[1] "Sunland Baptists Celebrate 46-Year Growth with Dedication of New Church This Sunday," *The Record-Ledger*, January 27, 1955.

[2] D.W. Griffith's *Abraham Lincoln*.

[3] *The Mark of Zorro* with Douglas Fairbanks.

[4] *It Happened One Night*, also starring Clark Cable.

[5] Murray, Marshall. Letter to Mary Lee Tiernan.

[6] Spelling of 'grandpa' used for Edgar.

[7] Murray, Marshall. Letter to Mary Lee Tiernan.

[8] In popular parlance, the lake was often referred to as Lancaster Lake—no 's'. The Lancasters, however, called the lake Lancasters Lake—with an 's,' but no apostrophe. The second edition defers to the family's spelling.

[9] Murray, Marshall. Letter to Mary Lee Tiernan.

[10] Wheeler, Sherrie. Personal interview.

[11] Gillan, Norman. Personal interview.

[12] Wheeler, Sherrie. Personal interview.

[13] Murray, Marshall. Letter to Mary Lee Tiernan.

Bibliography

"Baptist Church in Sunland Inspired by Boy's Defiance." *The Record-Ledger*, Historical & Progress Edition, May 21, 1953.

"Boating Is Good at Lancaster's Lake." *The Record-Ledger*, July 29, 1926.

"Church Bell Given by Mary Pickford." *The Record-Ledger*, January 27, 1955.

Coronado, Addie. Personal interview by Mary Lee Tiernan. July 16, 1999.

"Death Takes E.F. Lancaster, Valley Pioneer." *The Glendale NewsPress*, July 20, 1951.

"Early History of Sunland Baptist Church." Clippings file, Special Collections, Glendale Public Library.

"Early Sunland Landmark." Clippings file, Bolton Hall Museum.

"Edgar Lancaster Celebrates 90th Birthday." *The Record-Ledger*, October 28, 1948.

"Excavating for Sunland Church." *The Record-Ledger*, February 21, 1924.

Gillan, Norman. Personal interview by Mary Lee Tiernan. July 17, 1999.

Glover, Robert Lee. Funeral record. Bade Mortuary, Tujunga, CA.

Harn, Jay. "He Was Here in the Beginning." *The Record-Ledger*, February 12, 1986.

Hitt, Marlene. "Lancaster Lake the Best Place to Spend a Hot Summer Day." *The Foothill Leader*, March 14-15, 1998.

"Lancaster Lake." *The Record-Ledger*, Historical & Progress Edition, May 21, 1953.

"Lancaster Lake Is Now Sherman Grove Park." *The Record-Ledger*, September 30, 1954.

Lancaster Paul. Personal interview by Charles Miller, August 16, 1986.

"Many People Visit Lancaster Lake on the Fourth of July." *The Record-Ledger*, July 7, 1933.

"Marie Murray Recalls Days of Father's Lancaster Lake." *The Record-Ledger*, September 30, 1954.

McKee, Bob. "Sunland Recalled." *The Record-Ledger*, July 24, 1976.

Monroe, Irene. Personal interview by Mary Lee Tiernan. July 20, 1999.

Murray, Marshall. Letter to Mary Lee Tiernan. March 28, 2000.

Pozzo, Mary Lou. *Hollywood Comes to Sunland-Tujunga 1920-1995*. Tujunga, CA: Sunland-Tujunga Little Landers Historical Society. 1995.

Schell, Elizabeth Blumfield. "Early Memories of My Childhood." July 24, 1983.

"Sunland Baptists Celebrate 46-Year Growth with Dedication of New Church This Sunday." *The Record-Ledger*, January 27, 1955.

"Sunland School Nears 70 Years at Same Site." *The Record-Ledger*, July 3, 1975.

Sunland-Tujunga: Nestled between the Verdugo Hills and the San Gabriel Mts. The Sunland-Tujunga Chamber of Commerce. March, 1947.

Wheeler, Sherrie. Personal interview by Mary Lee Tiernan. July 28, 1999.

"Will Build Camp at Sunland." *The Record-Ledger*, August 6, 1925.

"Will Hold Picnic at Lancaster Lake." *The Record-Ledger*, August 19, 1926.

Wollard, Jack. Personal interview by Mary Lee Tiernan. July 17, 1999.

The Early History of Sunland, California

8 Volume Series
Also available as ebooks

Vol. 1 *Hotels for the Hopeful* Land promoters of the 1880s promised a perfect life of health, wealth, and pleasure. Although their promises fell short of reality, the village did grow and prosper in the hands of farmers.

Vol. 2 *The Roscoe Robbers and the Sensational Train Robbery of 1894* Two robbers posed as passengers to flag down the train. When the engineer recognized danger, he opened the throttle and sped past. The bandits threw the spur switch, and the train careened full speed off the tracks.

Vol. 3 *The Parson and His Cemetery* Parson Wornum was so loved that when he died, the whole village attended his funeral. Years of neglect of his cemetery spelled disaster in 1978 when heavy rains tore open graves and washed bodies down the hillside.

Vol. 4 *From Crackers to Coal Oil* When a student pulled out his gun and laid it on his desk, the tiny one-room school found itself needing a new teacher. That brought Virginia Newcomb, a romance, and a new family that helped to develop the town, leaving behind a detailed account of pioneer life in a small village.

Vol. 5 *He Never Came Home* Joe Ardizzone, a local grape-grower, doubled as a hit-man for the Mafia. During Prohibition, Joe's bootlegging activities caught him in the middle of in-house quarreling. In 1931, he left on a short trip and disappeared into the pages of history.

Vol. 6 *Lancasters Lake* When Edgar Lancaster dredged the swamp on his land, he created a lake which became a treasured landmark. For 25 years, visitors flocked to its cool shores, and Hollywood used the lake as a set location for some of its early movies.

Vol. 7 *Living in Big Tujunga Canyon* Early settlers, like the Johnson family, found their way into the canyon, a dense woodland bristling with wildlife. 50 years later, the Webber family faced the wrath of the river now winding down a denuded mountainside.

Vol. 8 *From Whence They Came* The Land Boom of the 1880s brought immigrants from around the world. Two generations of Blumfields survived the difficulties of farming and water shortages through industry and imagination.

www.ingramcontent.com/pod-product-compliance
Lightning Source LLC
Chambersburg PA
CBHW061348040426
42444CB00011B/3143